LET'S LEARN ABOUT...
THE OCEAN

PROJECT BOOK

CBEEBIES

K1

Pearson Education Limited
KAO Two, KAO Park, Harlow, Essex, CM17 9NA, England
and Associated Companies around the world

© Pearson Education Limited 2020

The right of Rhiannon S. Ball to be identified as author of this Work has been asserted by them in accordance with the Copyright, Designs and Patents Act 1988.

All rights reserved; no part of this publication may be reproduced, stored in a retrieval system, or transmitted in any form or by any means, electronic, mechanical, photocopying, recording, or otherwise without the prior written permission of the Publishers

First published 2020

ISBN: 978-1-292-33455-4

Set in Mundo Sans
Printed in China SWTC/01

Acknowledgements
The publishers and author(s) would like to thank the following people and institutions for their feedback and comments during the development of the material: Marcos Mendonça, Leandra Dias, Viviane Kirmeliene, Simara H. Dal'Alba, Mônica Bicalho and GB Editorial. The publishers would also like to thank all the teachers who contributed to the development of *Let's learn about...*: Adriano de Paula Souza, Aline Ramos Teixeira Santo, Aline Vitor Rodrigues Pina Pereira, Ana Paula Gomez Montero, Anna Flávia Feitosa Passos, Camila Jarola, Celiane Junker Silva, Edegar França Junior, Fabiana Reis Yoshio, Fernanda de Souza Thomaz, Luana da Silva, Michael Iacovino Luidvinavicius, Munique Dias de Melo, Priscila Rossatti Duval Ferreira Neves, Sandra Ferito, and schools that took part in Construindo Juntos.

Author Acknowledgements
Rhiannon S. Ball

Image Credit(s):
BBC Worldwide Learning: 9, 11, 15, 17, 19, 21, 23, 35; **Pearson Education Ltd:** Silva Serviços de Educação 7, 9, 9, 11, 13, 13, 13, 13, 13, 15, 17, 19, 19, 19, 19, 21, 21, 21, 21, 23, 25, 25, 25, 25, 25, 25, 27, 27, 27, 29, 29, 29, 29, 31, 33, 35, 51, 51, 51, 51, 51, 51, 53, 53, 53, 53, 53; **Shutterstock.com:** BudOlga 5, Codesyn 51, Moomchak V. Design 5, Puslatronik 5

Illustration Acknowledgements
Illustrated by Filipe Laurentino and Silva Serviços de Educação.

Cover illustration © Filipe Laurentino

CONTENTS

LOOK AND MATCH. COLOR.

LOOK, THINK, AND DRAW.

LOOK, THINK, AND STICK.

FIND AND CIRCLE. COUNT.

LOOK, COUNT, AND MATCH. 3

1   2   3   4   5

LOOK, THINK, AND DRAW.

LOOK, THINK, AND STICK.

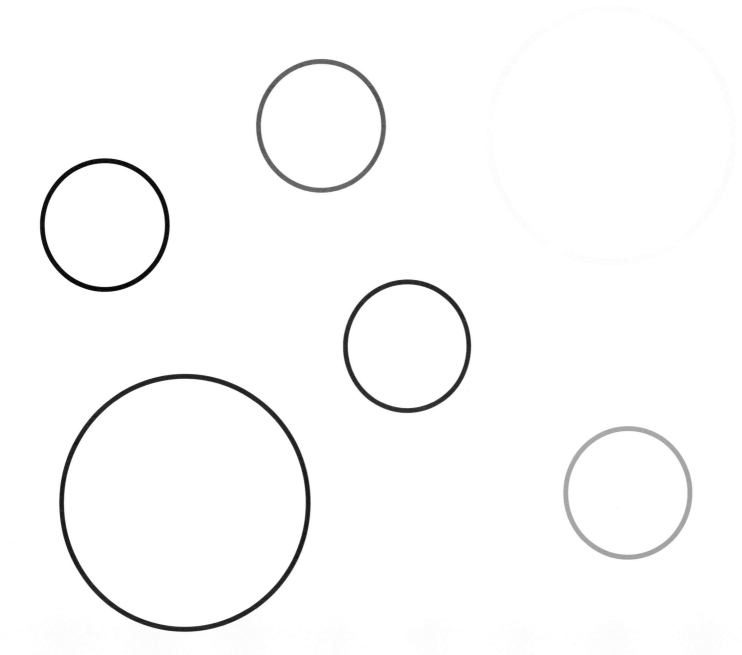

LOOK, THINK, AND DRAW.

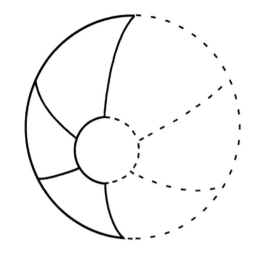

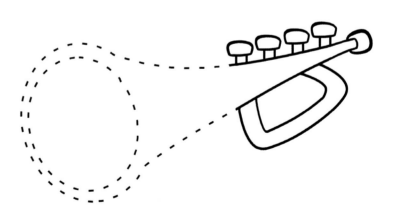

LOOK, COUNT, AND MATCH.

1

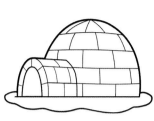 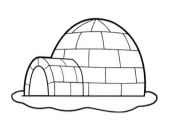 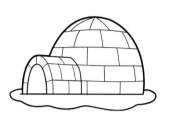

2

3

4

5

LOOK, THINK, AND DRAW.

LOOK, THINK, DRAW, AND MATCH.

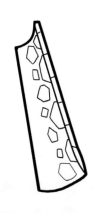

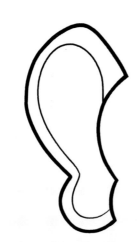

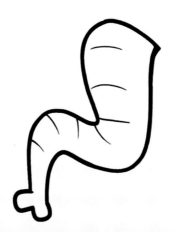

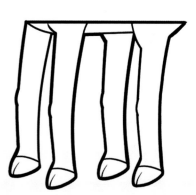

LOOK, FIND, AND STICK.

LOOK, THINK, AND DRAW.

LOOK, FIND, AND DRAW.

CIRCLE, COUNT, AND CHECK. 3

LOOK, THINK, AND STICK.

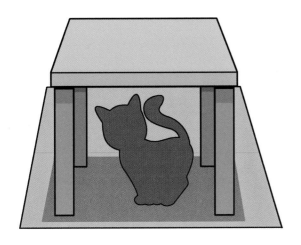

DRAWING

DRAW.

DRAW.

DRAW.

DRAW.

STICKERS